J B King
Sanford, William R.
Richard King : courageous
   Texas cattleman

$21.26
ocn765881458
Library ed.          08/05/2013

Courageous Heroes of the American West

# Richard King
## Courageous Texas Cattleman

*William R. Sanford and Carl R. Green*

**Enslow Publishers, Inc.**
40 Industrial Road
Box 398
Berkeley Heights, NJ 07922
USA

http://www.enslow.com

Original edition published as *Richard King: Texas Cattle Rancher* in 1997.

**Library of Congress Cataloging-in-Publication Data**

Sanford, William R. (William Reynolds), 1927–
  Richard King : courageous Texas cattleman / William R. Sanford and Carl R. Green.
      p. cm. — (Courageous heroes of the American West)
  "Original edition published as Richard King : Texas cattle rancher in 1997"—T.p. verso.
  Includes index.
  ISBN 978-0-7660-4003-8
  1. King, Richard, 1824–1885—Juvenile literature. 2. Ranchers—Texas—Biography—Juvenile
literature. 3. Ranch life—Texas—History—19th century—Juvenile literature. 4. Cattle trade—
Texas—History—19th century—Juvenile
literature. 5. Texas—Biography—Juvenile literature. I. Green, Carl R. II. Title.
  F391.K535S26 2013
  976.4'05092—dc23
  [B]
                                    2011048164

Future editions:
Paperback ISBN 978-1-4644-0088-9
ePUB ISBN 978-1-4645-0995-7
PDF ISBN 978-1-4646-0995-4

Printed in the United States of America

032012 Lake Book Manufacturing, Inc., Melrose Park, IL

10 9 8 7 6 5 4 3 2 1

**To Our Readers:** We have done our best to make sure all Internet addresses in this book were active
and appropriate when we went to press. However, the author and the Publisher have no control over
and assume no liability for, the material available on those Internet sites or on other Web sites they may
link to. Any comments or suggestions can be sent by e-mail to comments@enslow.com or to the address
on the back cover.

♻ Enslow Publishers, Inc., is committed to printing our books on recycled paper. The paper in every
book contains 10% to 30% post-consumer waste (PCW). The cover board on the outside of each book
contains 100% PCW. Our goal is to do our part to help young people and the environment too!

**Illustration Credits:** AP Images / Paul Iverson, pp. 42, 43; © 2012 Clipart.com, a division of Getty
Images, pp. 14, 39; Enslow Publishers, Inc., p. 20; © Enslow Publishers, Inc. / Paul Daly, p. 1;
The Granger Collection, NYC, p. 28; Library of Congress Prints and Photographs, pp. 7, 11, 34, 36;
Shutterstock.com, p. 24; Courtesy Texas State Library, from *Dictionary of American Portraits*, Dover
Publications, Inc., 1967, p. 32; Courtesy of the University of Texas Libraries, The University of Texas
at Austin, p. 19.

**Cover Illustration:** © Enslow Publishers, Inc. / Paul Daly.

# Contents

## Authors' Note

Richard King was a penniless steamboat pilot when he first came to Texas. After the Mexican War, he purchased a boat and went into business for himself. A few years later, he threw himself into the task of building a successful ranch. The obstacles were many. King had to carve his ranch from a hostile land of sand, brush, and broiling heat. As if nature were not challenge enough, he also had to fight off outlaws and find markets for his cattle. With skill, perseverance, and courage, he built a cattle empire that still endures. This is his true story.

# Chapter 1

# A Cattleman's Dream

Texas has always inspired grand dreams. In the late 1860s, Captain Richard King was one of the dreamers. The Civil War was over, and there were fortunes to be made in the Lone Star State. Although the steamboat pilot turned rancher owned thousands of acres, he longed for more. Someday, he vowed, he would own all of South Texas from the Nueces River to the Rio Grande.

Thousands of longhorns grazed on Richard's Santa Gertrudis Ranch. If he found a market for those fast-growing steers, he could buy more land. His chance came with the rising demand for beef in the northern states. A steer worth $11 in Texas sold for $32 in Chicago. The problem was one of transport. Shipping cattle by boat was too costly. The railroad was cheaper, but the nearest railhead lay far to the north. Richard would have to drive his longhorns overland.

The numbers were daunting. A thousand miles of prairie lay between the ranch and the Kansas railheads. Moving at a top speed of twelve miles a day, a cattle drive would take at least three months. If the cattle lost weight, their price dropped. Richard had to plan his drives for months when the grass was good.

Richard sent his *vaqueros* (cowboys) north to Abilene, Kansas, with a herd in 1870. Dozens of trail drives soon followed. A cowboy wrote in 1882: "On reaching Santa Gertrudis ranch, [we] learned that three trail herds, of over three thousand head each had already started. . . . Four more were ready to follow." During the next fifteen years, Richard sent more than a hundred thousand steers up the trail. Most were destined for the Midwestern slaughterhouses. Others stocked new ranches in Wyoming and Montana.

Captain King helped set the pattern for all the cattle drives to come. His trail boss and ten vaqueros herded the half-wild longhorns. A cook drove a chuck wagon stuffed with bedrolls and supplies. A wrangler took charge of the extra horses. A typical drive started in February with a roundup. Herds ranged in size from one thousand to four thousand head. By March, the drive was underway. Spring grasses fattened the longhorns as they moved up the trail.

Cowboys round up stray cattle during the long drive to markets in the Midwest. In the 1860s, Richard King sent his longhorn steers over a thousand miles of prairie from the King Ranch to the Kansas railheads in Abilene. Captain King's success helped set the pattern for all the cattle drives to come.

Most ranchers paid their trail bosses about $100 a month. Richard had a better plan. His trail bosses took more care with the cattle because they were partners in the drive. Before heading north, a trail boss signed a note for the herd at its Texas value. To that figure Richard added the value of the horses, wagons, and other equipment. Then he gave the trail boss the cash needed to pay wages and purchase supplies. After the cattle were sold and the expenses deducted, the trail boss shared in the profits.

On one drive in 1875, trail boss John Fitch signed for 4,737 cattle and 137 horses. Four months later, Fitch sold the cattle for $18 a head. His share of the profits came to $5,366. Most men worked for years to earn that much money. Raising the cattle had cost Richard less than two dollars a head. He collected $61,886, of which more than $50,000 was profit.

On the King Ranch, only the best cattle went to market. Undersized and poorly developed steers were killed for their hides and tallow. To improve his longhorns, Richard brought in Durham bulls from Kentucky. His goal was to produce a steer with a longhorn's toughness and a Durham's bulk. By the 1920s, those early efforts would lead to a productive new breed, the Santa Gertrudis.

In pursuing his dream, Richard King invented modern ranching. Before he came along, farmers tended to raise cattle as a sideline. In the cities, fresh meat was a luxury few could afford. The King Ranch turned ranching into a big business. It also helped turn Americans into a nation of meat eaters.

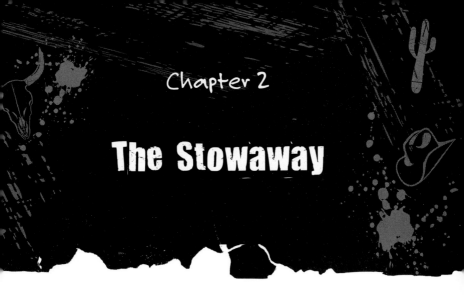

# Chapter 2

# The Stowaway

The story of the King Ranch begins on the high seas. In 1835, the sailing ship *Desdemona* was four days out of New York. When the crew checked the hold, they found an eleven-year-old stowaway. The sailors hauled the frightened boy to the deck. Under the captain's stern gaze, he told his story.

His name was Richard King. He said he was born in New York City on July 10, 1824. His immigrant Irish parents lived in poverty. Neither then nor later did Richard reveal their names. When he was nine, young Richard was apprenticed to a jeweler. Instead of teaching him the trade, the jeweler treated Richard like a servant. The boy swept, cleaned, and scrubbed. He also took care of the jeweler's baby.

Boredom led to rebellion. Richard fled the jeweler's house and ran to the waterfront. He had learned about stowaways from friendly roustabouts. That night, one of the men helped him hide on the *Desdemona*. Since then, he had spent four days and nights in the dark hold. His only food had been the sack of bread he brought with him. Was he telling the truth? The record gives us no other data on Richard's early life. No one from his family ever claimed him as kin.

Richard begged the captain not to send him back. He was willing to work for his passage, he said. The captain looked down at the small, smudged face. He saw a square jaw, dark hair, and deep blue eyes. The appeal in those eyes touched his heart. He put Richard to work as his cabin boy. His faith was not misplaced. Richard was a hard worker and a quick learner.

Some days later, the *Desdemona* docked in Mobile, Alabama. The captain, now a good friend, found young Richard a new job. For the next two years, the boy sailed southern rivers on Captain Joe Holland's steamboat. In 1837, Holland chose Richard to be his cub. As a cub, the boy was in training to be a river pilot. The thirteen-year-old had to learn every bend, sandbar, and snag on the Alabama River. In his spare time, the kindly Holland taught Richard how to read.

Along with taking his turn at the wheel, Richard helped keep the ship's books. Holland was impressed by the boy's flair for numbers. He sent his cub to his

Richard King spent much of his childhood on the river, where he worked on steamboats. After Captain Joe Holland chose the boy to be his cub, he trained Richard to be a riverboat pilot.

family in Connecticut to go to school. Richard starred in the classroom, but he missed the rough-and-tumble life of the river. He stuck it out for eight months; then he left. It was his first and last brush with school.

Richard headed for Florida in the midst of the Second Seminole War. Tough, reliable sailors were in demand. In 1841, he was on the *Ocochohee* when the Seminole chief, Hospetarke, came aboard. The Seminole hoped to talk the army out of whiskey and supplies. Instead, he and his warriors were taken prisoner. The arrest helped bring the war to a close.

By 1843, young Richard King had grown and matured. Somewhere along the way, he had been granted his pilot's license. At nineteen, he was square-jawed, well-muscled, and tall for the times at five feet, eleven inches. When provoked, he could turn the air purple with cusswords. That made the friendship he formed with Mifflin Kenedy something of a surprise. Kenedy, master of the *Champion*, was a well-educated, soft-spoken Quaker. He also was seven years older than Richard.

In 1846, Kenedy sailed the *Champion* upriver to Pittsburgh, Pennsylvania, for an overhaul. The United States went to war with Mexico that same year. Both countries were claiming a large chunk of southern Texas. In August, Kenedy wrote to Richard with exciting news.

Kenedy's new command, the *Corvette*, was hauling supplies for the U.S. Army. That meant sailing up a long, twisting river called the Rio Grande. For more than a thousand miles, the river marked the border between the United States and Mexico. Sandbars, sharp bends, and shifting currents tested a pilot's skill to the utmost. Kenedy told Richard he was just the man for the job.

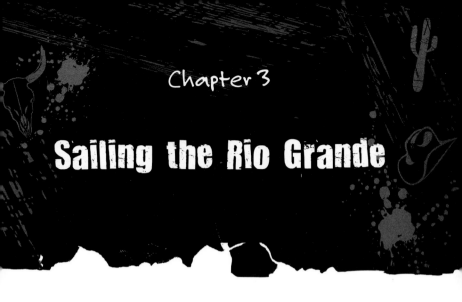

# Chapter 3

# Sailing the Rio Grande

Richard's ship dropped anchor near the mouth of the Rio Grande in May 1847. A sandbar blocked access to the river. Crewmen rowed their young passenger to the shore. Richard carried only a seabag. The canvas bag held all that he owned.

A few wooden shanties stood on the Texas side of the river. The local Texans called it Boca del Rio (Mouth of the River). Across the river lay the lawless Mexican town of Bagdad. Travelers found cheap whiskey, crooked card games, and sudden death there. Richard, however, loved a good brawl. He enjoyed his visits to those mean streets.

Richard was content to wait for Mifflin Kenedy, who was upriver with the *Corvette*. The old-timers he met at Boca del Rio filled him in on the war. The United States claimed that the Rio Grande was the

In May 1846, Zachary Taylor, seated on his white horse, led U.S. troops into battle during the Mexican-American War. During the conflict, the U.S. Army hired Richard King as a steamboat pilot to help ferry much-needed supplies to the American soldiers.

border between Mexico and Texas. Mexico insisted it lay 130 miles north, at the Nueces River. U.S. Army troops marched in to enforce their country's claim.

In May 1846, the two armies had clashed. Zachary Taylor led the U.S. troops. They drove the Mexicans back across the Rio Grande. Four months later, Taylor crossed into Mexico. His triumph at Monterrey stamped out Mexican resistance in the north.

Taylor's army needed a constant stream of supplies. Steamboats were the best way to transport food and guns. The army hired Richard as second pilot on the

*Colonel Cross*. Captain Kenedy soon moved Richard to the *Corvette* and promoted him to first pilot. Richard's pay doubled, from $60 to $120 a month.

The *Corvette* was used to transport supplies. The shallow-draft boat needed only twenty inches of water under its hull when it was empty. Fully loaded for the trip up the Rio Grande, it floated clear on thirty inches of muddy river water. Even so, the *Corvette* scraped the sandbar at the river's mouth. Three miles to the north, a narrow channel led into a sheltered bay. There, at Point Isabel, workers unloaded the seagoing ships, which could not cross the sandbar.

The *Corvette* docked, and workmen filled its hold with supplies. Then Kenedy headed the steamboat upriver. Richard's task was to learn each twist and turn of the 250-mile route. Above Reynosa, he saw the Wild Horse Desert for the first time. Forty-two miles up the river, the *Corvette* unloaded at Carmargo. From there, mule trains took the supplies to Taylor at Monterrey. The end of the *Corvette*'s run came at Mier, thirty miles farther on.

All along the river, militia troops stood guard. Privates earned only $7 a month. Many served a few months and left without seeing action. Others fell ill and died, victims of the heat and bad water.

By contrast, the *Corvette* was a floating palace. Richard slept on a soft bed in a clean cabin. The cook fed him hearty meals.

Despite the comforts, Richard seldom relaxed. The Rio Grande's muddy waters hid a long list of dangers. Hidden snags lay in wait, ready to rip open the hull. The current could push a careless pilot into the bank as he rounded a bend. The result often was a smashed paddle wheel. Too much steam could cause a boiler to explode. The young pilot met each challenge. He brought the *Corvette* safely home from each trip.

Mexico City fell to the U.S. Army in September 1847. The diplomats took over and signed a peace treaty early in 1848. Richard ferried some of the departing American soldiers downriver in his first command, the *Colonel Cross*. As the troops thinned out, however, the demand for steamboats fell sharply. Richard lost his job with the army, but he stayed in Texas. He had money in his pocket. It was time to start his own business.

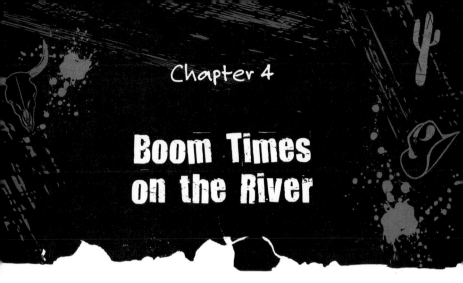

# Chapter 4

## Boom Times on the River

The Army beached its Rio Grande steamboats after the war ended. Richard kept a keen eye on the surplus boats. Once they went on sale, he planned to buy one.

While he waited, Richard opened an inn at Boca del Rio. As an innkeeper, he was a jack-of-all-trades. He tended bar, made beds, and joked with his customers. The inn drew a lively crowd. Keeping drunks in line kept the hard-fisted captain in fighting shape.

In April 1849, the army put eleven steamboats up for sale. Richard bought the *Colonel Cross*. The boat was badly battered. Even so, at $750 it was a bargain. The army had paid $14,000 for it. Richard closed his inn. He hired a crew and made a number of badly-needed repairs. Then he began hauling cargo for the merchants in Matamoros.

The *Colonel Cross* carried wool, beef hides, lead, silver, and gold downriver. On his return trips, Richard hauled hardware, cloth, tobacco, and other items that were destined for sale in northern Mexico. His crew unloaded the goods on the Texas side of the river. From there, the merchants smuggled them into Mexico. Customs officers took bribes to look the other way.

Richard soon had all the business he could handle. Because he was captain, pilot, and clerk, his costs were low. By contrast, Charles Stillman's steamboats lost money on almost every trip. Early in 1850, Stillman asked Mifflin Kenedy to become his partner. After dabbling in overland trade, Kenedy was eager to return to the river. One of his first acts was to talk Richard into joining them. If Captain King could not make steamboats pay, no one could. Richard promptly signed on as a partner.

Stillman agreed to finance a new fleet. Richard took charge of designing two of the new boats. The *Grampus* would be a big side-wheeler. Its job was to move large payloads from Point Isabel to Boca del Rio. For river traffic, he designed a powerful flat-bottomed stern-wheeler. Fully loaded, the *Comanche* could float in less than two feet of water. Kenedy made the long trip to Pittsburgh to order the new boats.

Mifflin Kenedy, pictured here, went into the steamboat business in Texas with his old friend, Richard King.

On a gloomy day in February, Richard steered the *Colonel Cross* upstream. The balky old steamboat seemed to fight him at every turn. At last, he reached the Brownsville waterfront. He was in a foul mood as he pointed the steamboat toward its mooring. As Richard neared the dock, he saw that a ship called the *Whiteville* was blocking his way. Swearing loudly, he backed off. Then, calling on all his skill, he shoehorned the *Cross* into a nearby slip.

A man at dockside told him that the *Whiteville* was now a houseboat. The town's new preacher and his family lived there. While Richard chewed on the news,

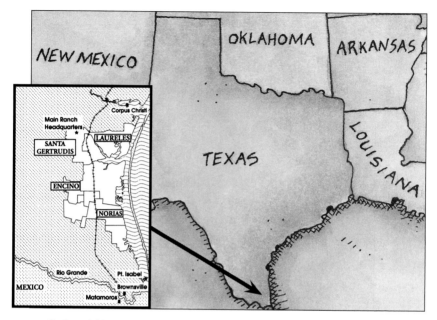

Richard King captained steamboats carrying goods for trade on the Rio Grande, the natural border separating Texas and Mexico. Texas soon became Richard's home. The inset map shows the King Ranch and other important places in his life.

a new voice caught his ear. A pretty young woman was calling from the houseboat. In a clear, angry voice, she told Richard what she thought of his foul language. His ship, she added, was just as filthy. For once, Richard was speechless. Here was a woman with spirit. Here was a woman he could love.

Richard asked Kenedy about the new preacher's daughter. He learned that she was seventeen-year-old Henrietta Chamberlain. Richard put on his finest suit and went to church. For him, Wednesday prayer meetings were special. That was when brown-eyed Henrietta sang in the choir. Perhaps she welcomed his pursuit. However, her father, the Reverend Hiram Chamberlain, preferred her gentlemen suitors.

Richard spent his days building warehouses and docks. The arrival of the new ships in August 1850 doubled his workload. When the construction was done, he took command of the *Grampus*. The sturdy side-wheeler shuttled cargo from Point Isabel to new docks ten miles upriver. From there, Kenedy hauled the cargo to Matamoros in the *Comanche*.

The efficient new steamboats allowed the partners to lower their rates. In less than two years, they controlled the river trade. The fleet grew to five boats. Each partner was banking $10,000 a year. Richard began looking for new investments.

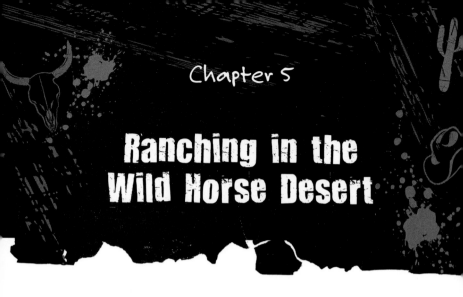

# Chapter 5

# Ranching in the Wild Horse Desert

In April 1852, Richard saddled up and rode northward. He and a group of friends were headed toward Corpus Christi. The main lure was the Lone Star State Fair, but Richard also wanted to see the grasslands of the Wild Horse Desert. Mexicans had another name for the region. They called it El Desierto de los Muertos—the Desert of the Dead.

At first, the route led across endless miles of sand. Then, as the party pushed north, the landscape changed. Dunes gave way to a trackless sea of grass. Islands of mesquite, oak, and hackberry trees dotted the plain. Herds of wild mustangs and longhorn cattle raced away as the men approached. Thirst kept the animals on the move. Water was in short supply.

At the fair, Richard spent some time with Gideon "Legs" Lewis of the Texas Rangers. In time, the talk turned to cattle and ranching. Lewis was convinced that the region was a rancher's paradise. He suggested they go into the cattle business. Richard would put up the money, and Lewis would work the ranch and guard against bandits.

The two men shook hands on the deal. On his way north, Richard had camped near tree-shaded Santa Gertrudis Creek. He chose this spot as the site of his ranch. Legs hired a work crew. The men built huts, a corral, and a stockade. Then they rode out to round up herds of wild horses and cattle.

Richard tracked down the Mexican owners. Most were glad to sell. Their lands north of the Rio Grande now lay in a foreign country. In 1853, Richard bought 15,500 acres for $300—less than two cents an acre. A year later, he purchased an adjoining 53,000 acres for $1,800. His friends told him he had paid too much. Richard ignored them and plowed more money into the ranch.

In Mexico, Richard studied the self-contained ranches called *haciendas*. The landowners lived in large, fortresslike houses. Nearby were clusters of the workers' homes and other outbuildings. The vaqueros worked livestock from horseback. Richard decided to build his Santa Gertrudis Ranch to that model.

Richard King used his steamboat profits to start a cattle ranching business with Gideon "Legs" Lewis. Richard's cattle-buying trips usually ended in the purchase of more longhorn steers.

During one cattle-buying trip, Richard visited a drought-stricken Mexican village. After he bought their steers, he saw how poor the people were. "Come work for me," he told them. "You can build a new life on my land." More than a hundred men, women, and children followed him north. True to his word, Richard always treated his workers fairly. In return, *los Kineños* (the King People) served *el Patron* (the boss) loyally.

Along with the ranch, Richard had steamboats to run. He also made time for his courtship of Henrietta. After four years, his efforts paid off. The Reverend

Hiram Chamberlain at last agreed to the marriage. On December 10, 1854, the couple said their vows in his Brownsville church. Then they boarded Richard's new stagecoach to spend their honeymoon at the ranch.

Armed vaqueros escorted the stagecoach on the 120-mile trip. When the newlyweds arrived, the main ranch house was only half built. They set up temporarily in a small adobe house. Space was limited. Henrietta had to hang her pots on the outside wall. Despite the hardships, she fell in love with the ranch. Later, she wrote: "I doubt if it falls to the lot of any bride to have had so happy a honeymoon. On horseback we roamed the broad prairies. When I grew tired . . . I would take my siesta under the shade of the mesquite tree."

When Richard was away, los Kineños guarded Henrietta closely. They loved *la Patrona*. In her calm, efficient way, she nursed the sick and helped the needy. In time, Richard built a one-room school on the ranch. It was Henrietta who taught the lessons.

In April 1855, a jealous husband shot Legs Lewis. Richard had to buy his partner's share from his heirs. Money was flowing out, but Richard refused to worry. "Land and livestock have a way of increasing in value," he told Kenedy. "But boats—they have a way of wrecking, decaying, falling apart."

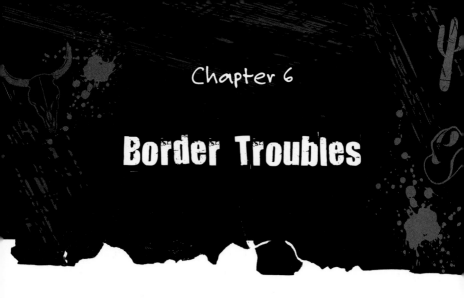

# Chapter 6

# Border Troubles

Richard told his vaqueros to breed only strong, beefy longhorns. The cowboys picked the strongest bulls to breed with the best cows. Weaker animals were slaughtered for hides and tallow. Season by season, his methods produced better steers. In the meantime, the Kings bought a house in Brownsville. There, in the spring of 1856, Henrietta gave birth to a daughter. The proud parents named her Henrietta, but called her Nettie.

That fall, Richard met Colonel Robert E. Lee. The dignified Virginian was serving at Fort Brown. He soon became a frequent guest at the ranch. Lee knew land and livestock as well as he knew soldiering. It was Lee who told his younger friend, "Buy land; and never sell." Richard never forgot that advice.

The Kings often camped out on their trips to the ranch. One night, a Mexican appeared and asked to join them. Richard said yes, and he sent the man to gather firewood. Moments later, Henrietta screamed, "Captain King! Behind you!" Quick as a cat, Richard turned and grabbed the stranger's arm. As he twisted, a knife fell to the ground. Instead of killing the man, Richard booted him out of his camp.

Trouble was no stranger to the border region. In February 1859, two events added to the turmoil. First, Mexico set up a six-mile free-trade zone along the Rio Grande. Then a bumbling American general pulled out all U.S. Army troops along the border. Like hungry vultures, smugglers and rustlers poured in. Texans complained that one of the worst cutthroats was a Mexican general named Juan Cortina. His San José ranch, they said, was little more than a den of thieves. Many of the Mexicans who lived along the border disagreed. They thought of Cortina as a folk hero.

One day in July, Cortina and a few of his men rode into Brownsville. The town had grown up on land he claimed as his own. When Cortina saw the town marshal mistreat a Mexican drunk, hard words led to gunplay. Cortina shot the marshal and freed the prisoner. Then he rode back to his ranch.

Three months later, Cortina, at the head of a small army, stormed into Brownsville. A brief gunfight left

Masked cattle rustlers pose for a photo during the 1880s. Cattle rustlers and bandits, led by the Mexican general Juan Cortina, became a serious problem for Richard King and other ranchers.

five Texans dead or dying. Cortina was about to burn the town when help arrived—from Mexico. A Mexican officer led a cavalry troop across the river. The officer, who was Cortina's cousin, talked his kinsman into sparing the town.

The raid marked the outbreak of the First Cortina War. Cortina urged his men to attack all Texans. Along with burning and looting, his bands indulged in an orgy of killing. A government report noted: "Old and young were . . . dragged at the hooves of horses, burned and flayed alive, shot to death or cut to pieces with knives."

The reign of terror brought help at last. Army troops arrived in December, along with a unit of Texas Rangers. The small force drove Cortina away from Brownsville. The bandit chief then turned to new targets. His raids brought in a second Ranger force under John S. "Rip" Ford. Richard King supplied Ford with provisions and information. In a series of bloody clashes, Ford drove Cortina's raiders back into Mexico.

The fighting hurt Richard's businesses. On the river, traffic stopped for five months. Out on the ranch, rustlers drove off thousands of longhorns. It is unclear where Richard was at this time, but he hurried back to the ranch to strengthen its defenses.

By June 1860, Richard was filing claims against the government. He argued that the army had been lax in leaving the border open to attack. His lawyer asked for more than $250,000 in damages. Washington turned a deaf ear to the claims.

By this time, the nation stood at the brink of civil war. Richard hurried to prepare for the conflict. He and Kenedy placed orders for new steamboats. They knew that freight traffic would boom during a war. To raise capital, Richard took Kenedy in as a partner in his ranch. They named the new firm R. King & Company. The Civil War was only four months away.

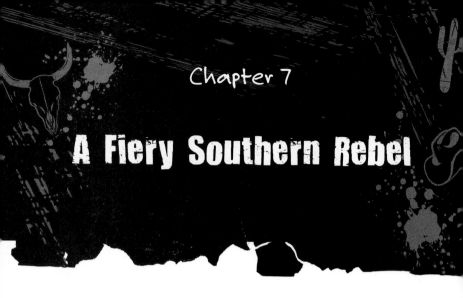

# Chapter 7

# A Fiery Southern Rebel

In February 1861, Texas voted to join the Confederate States of America. The U.S. Army withdrew from the rebel state. A force of 1,500 Confederates took its place along the Rio Grande. In April, Southern troops fired on Fort Sumter, South Carolina. The Civil War had begun.

Richard King was a loyal Texan. For most men, serving the cause meant joining the army. Richard performed a greater service. His cattle fed rebel troops. His steamboats carried Southern cotton into Mexican ports. On the return trip, they hauled guns and medicines. War or no war, Richard did not lose his business sense. He charged $5 in gold for each bale of cotton he shipped.

At first, Southern cotton moved freely to overseas markets. The Union responded with a naval blockade.

Early in 1862, a U.S. warship arrived to patrol the Texas coast. Richard and his partners promptly registered their steamboats in Mexico. Because Mexico was neutral, the Union could not fire on these ships. The blockade closed the South's other ports one by one. Only the South's back door along the Rio Grande stayed open.

Cotton rolled in from four rebel states. The Santa Gertrudis Ranch served as a shipping and storage point. Bales were marked with the brands of neutral countries. Union watchdogs were powerless to stop the flow of cotton to waiting English ships. The South bought supplies with its cotton money. One shipment the steamboats carried was labeled "Bean Flour." In fact, the barrels held much-needed gunpowder.

The King family often stayed at the Santa Gertrudis Ranch. By this time, Henrietta had given birth to two more children, Ella and Richard II. On April 29, 1862, Alice Gertrudis King was born.

A severe drought struck Texas in 1863. The level of the river fell, stranding the steamboats. Richard rounded up oxen, mules, and carts. His drivers hauled the heavy bales of cotton over rutted, dusty roads.

Richard's company signed a contract to supply the rebel troops stationed along the border. The partners

During the Civil War, Richard King signed a contract to supply Confederate troops who were stationed along the border. He used the profits to buy more land for the King Ranch.

took payment in bales of cotton, which they sold to British mill owners. Richard used his share of the profits to buy more land. He added the Agua Dulce and Laureles grants to the Santa Gertrudis Ranch. The ranch now sprawled across some three hundred thousand acres.

In November 1863, seven thousand Union troops arrived off Point Isabel. Confederate general Hamilton Bee panicked. He ordered his men to set fire to the cotton stored in Brownsville, and then he withdrew. The fires spread and burned much of the town.

A month later, the Union general ordered Richard's arrest. Out at the ranch, a warning arrived just in time. Los Kineños were brave, but they could not fight off army troops. Richard had gone to Mexico to round up stolen livestock, leaving his pregnant wife behind. The Yankees, he reasoned, would not harm Henrietta.

That night, Union troops galloped up to the ranch house. A ranch hand tried to tell them that Richard was gone. One of the soldiers gunned him down. Angered by their quarry's escape, horsemen stormed into the living room. They smashed windows, mirrors, and china. Two days later, rumors of an approaching rebel relief column reached the ranch. The Yankee troops loaded up their loot and rode away.

Richard, still in Mexico, had his family moved to safety above the Nueces River. Two months later, Henrietta gave birth to their second son. The raid had not crushed her spirit. She named the boy for the South's foremost general, her friend Robert E. Lee.

Another old friend returned to action about this time. Rip Ford led an attack against Union troops around Brownsville. In July 1864, the Yankees pulled back to Boca del Rio. Thanks to Richard's wagon trains and steamboats, Ford's troops were well supplied.

Although many Civil War battles took place in the East, Texans saw their share of the fighting. Richard King was forced to move his family to safety above the Nueces River. This illustration depicts a naval battle in Galveston Bay off the coast of Texas. The Union navy destroyed its own vessel, the *Westfield*, rather than let the ship fall into rebel hands.

In May 1865, the two sides fought the final battle of the Civil War at Palmito Ranch, Texas. The war in the east had ended a month earlier when General Lee surrendered at Appomattox.

Richard stayed in Matamoros and waited. He had built his fortune, but he had been fighting on the losing side. Would peace allow a return to business as usual?

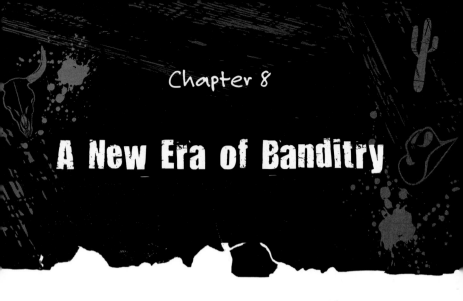

# Chapter 8

# A New Era of Banditry

The Union set up Reconstruction governments in the defeated Southern states. The new state governments were run by Northern carpet-baggers. These migrant politicians used their power mostly to enrich themselves. They also gave newly freed African-American slaves the right to vote and hold office.

Richard King was not allowed to reenter public life until he was pardoned. Luckily, he had friends in high places. President Andrew Johnson issued his pardon late in 1865.

Before long, Richard and Mifflin Kenedy were back in the steamboat business. They called the firm King, Kenedy & Company. Using wartime profits, the partners bought four new steamboats. Their fleet soon regained control of traffic on the Rio Grande.

After the Civil War, the Union installed Reconstruction governments in the defeated Southern states. Northern politicians, whom the Southerners called "carpetbaggers," controlled these new governments. This political cartoon published in *Harper's Weekly* on November 9, 1872, pokes fun at a greedy, southbound carpetbagger.

The Reconstruction government disbanded the Texas Rangers, and army troops took their place. The slow-moving units failed badly as border guards. Texas longhorns vanished into Mexico by the tens of thousands. One rustler was heard to brag, "The *Gringos* are raising cows for me."

Juan Cortina returned. Posing as an honest rancher, he signed contracts to deliver cattle to foreign buyers. Then he sent his bandits into Texas to steal the steers. At the Santa Gertrudis, los Kineños carried repeating rifles, and a brass cannon stood loaded and ready. Guards manned a lookout tower around the clock.

In three years, Richard lost thirty-three thousand cattle. He asked the state for help, but the governor refused. In 1867, Richard began to fence his huge ranch. At first, his crews put up wooden fences. After barbed wire appeared in 1874, the work went faster. In 1883 alone, the ranch ordered 190,000 pounds of barbed wire.

The postwar years brought other changes, too. As railroads were built, steamboat lines lost business. Richard and Kenedy sold their last boats in 1874. On the ranch, however, the yearly trail drives were paying off. The two partners also realized that the death of either man would create legal problems. By 1870, the two friends had divided the land and the cattle. Richard kept the northern half, and Kenedy settled on the Laureles grant.

On his trips to town, Richard's strongbox sometimes held $50,000. For safety's sake, he rode with an armed escort. Relay stations supplied him with fresh mounts. Even so, he barely survived an ambush in July 1872. A band of gunmen attacked his coach and riddled it with bullets. A passenger sitting next to him was shot and killed.

An army report stated: "The country between Corpus Christi and the Rio Grande . . . is full of armed bands of Mexicans. . . . A courier sent from King's ranch brings [news] that they are surrounded . . . and ask for aid." The army, tangled in red tape, did nothing. Legend says that los Kineños fought off the raiders. They sealed their triumph by hanging their captives.

The Texas Rangers were revived in 1874. Leander H. McNelly led the unit sent to the Wild Horse Desert. Richard greeted the Rangers warmly. Before they left, he replaced their tired nags with good saddle horses. Captain McNelly rode off on a big bay worth $500.

In June 1875, the Rangers pursued and shot a dozen bandits. As a lesson, McNelly dumped the bodies in the Brownsville public square. He and his men were tireless in their pursuit of rustlers. Sadly, some of the men they gunned down were innocent of any crime.

That fall, McNelly planned a raid on the rustlers' main base at Las Cuevas. The fact that the ranch was in Mexico did not bother him. He asked local army units to join him. Orders from headquarters held them back. In November 1875, the Rangers attacked—but hit the wrong ranch. With Las Cuevas alerted, McNelly pulled back. The Mexicans staged their own attack,

After the Civil War, the Texas Rangers did their best to keep the peace along the border. Men like this young Ranger crossed into Mexico and recovered some of Richard King's stolen longhorns.

but the sharpshooting Rangers drove them off. At last, their leader dead, the bandits asked for a truce. McNelly demanded the return of the stolen cattle. Thirty-five of the steers carried the King Ranch brand.

Richard was amazed when the Rangers delivered his longhorns. No one else had ever brought stolen cattle back from Mexico. His older daughters sent two big cakes to their guests. Their note read, *Compliments of the two Miss Kings to the McNelly Rangers.*

The rustling did not stop. Fewer steers, however, disappeared across the border. Thanks to the Rangers, many outlaws sought a safer way to make a living.

# Chapter 9

# "I Never Knew . . . a Better Man"

B y the time he turned fifty, Richard King was fast becoming a legend. Newspapers referred to him as the "King of Texas." At home, the always formal Henrietta addressed him as Captain King. Behind his back, friends called him Old Cap.

Wealth and fame did not go to the captain's head. Once, when a ranch hand complained that he was tired of being yelled at, Richard pulled off his hat. "Forget the riches and the captain title and let's fight," he barked. The two men traded punches for half an hour. Then, bloody and arm-weary, they shook hands. In 1881, the Texas Mexican railroad ran its first train from Corpus Christi to Laredo. Richard had been a driving force in building the railroad. To celebrate, he filled his private car with important guests. Then he spiked the lemonade. The leading citizens of South Texas were drunk and rowdy when the train reached Laredo.

Richard could be a hard man. He demanded a day's work for a day's pay, but he was not a skinflint. If a Kineño ran afoul of the law, the captain paid the bail. His greatest tenderness was reserved for his children. In a letter to Henrietta he wrote: "See that none of Papa's pets wants for anything money will buy."

It was Robert Lee who inherited his father's love of ranching. As part of his training, Lee was sent to school in St. Louis. He died there of pneumonia at age nineteen. His death nearly broke Richard's heart. For a while, he talked about selling. Buyers, however, balked at the asking price of $6.5 million.

Ella and Nettie married and settled in St. Louis. Alice was the only child left at home after Richard II married. As a wedding gift, Richard gave his son a forty-thousand-acre ranch. The Puerta de Agua Dulce was unlike the big ranch in one way. It had plenty of water.

Richard stood out in any crowd. Blue eyes blazed from his weathered face. A black beard covered his strong, square chin. He walked with a limp, the souvenir of a steamboat accident. Alice sometimes scolded her father for his careless dress. His wrinkled coat seldom matched his pants. If one pant leg was tucked into his dusty boots, the other often hung free.

At 614,140 acres, the King Ranch was almost as big as Rhode Island. Even so, Richard wanted more. He spelled this out to the lawyer hired to buy land for him. "Young man," the captain said, "the only thing I want to hear from you is when I can move my fences."

In 1881, Richard found a man who could take his place. After losing a law case, he hired the law firm

The King Ranch, at more than six hundred thousand acres, was almost as large as the state of Rhode Island. The cattle that grazed on the ranch were branded with Richard's famous Running W. Today, visitors to the King Ranch are greeted by the brand as they enter the front gate.

A cowboy moves a herd of cattle out of the feeding pens into a pasture on the King Ranch near Kingsville, Texas. The ranch still operates today and stands as a monument to the courageous man who founded it.

that had beaten him. Robert Kleberg drove to the ranch with his new boss that same night. Their arrival woke up Alice, who dressed and made coffee. Kleberg, Richard soon found, was a natural-born rancher. He also welcomed the young man's courtship of Alice. The couple became engaged in 1884.

By that time, Richard knew he was dying. The pain of his stomach cancer could no longer be deadened by whiskey. The birth of a grandson, Richard King III, brought a small measure of cheer. In January 1885, Richard left the ranch to be near his doctor in San Antonio. As the end drew near, the family gathered close. Richard signed his will. The brief document left everything to Henrietta. Death came twelve days later, on April 14, 1885.

Today, a strong and healthy King Ranch stands as Richard King's monument. His descendants have built well on the solid foundation he laid. That thought would have pleased the tough old steamboat captain. An elderly trail driver's tribute would have brought a smile, too. "I never knew a rougher man," Walter Billingsley said, "nor a better man."

# Glossary

**adobe**—A brick made of sun-dried straw and heavy clay. Also, a structure made with adobe bricks.

**apprentice**—Someone who learns a trade by working under the supervision of an experienced craftsperson.

**blockade**—The use of warships to prevent commerce from moving through an enemy's seaports.

**carpetbagger**—A Northerner who went south after the Civil War for political or financial gain.

**free-trade zone**—A border region where goods may be imported and exported without paying customs taxes.

**Gringos**—Mexican slang for a foreigner, particularly someone from the United States.

**hacienda**—Spanish for a large, self-contained ranch or plantation.

**longhorn cattle**—A traditional breed of cattle known for their long horns.

**los Kineños**—Spanish for "the King People"—the King Ranch's first Mexican workers and their descendants.

**militia**—Part-time soldiers who are called to duty in times of emergency.

**mustang**—A wild horse of the North American plains.

**pardon**—The act by a president or governor that grants legal forgiveness for a crime.

**pilot (maritime)**—A sailor who is licensed to steer ships through rivers and harbors.

**Quaker**—A member of a religious group known as the Society of Friends.

**Reconstruction**—The period after 1865 when Northern troops occupied the defeated states of the Confederacy.

**roustabout**—A dockworker who loads and unloads cargo from ships.

**side-wheeler**—A steamship with paddle wheels located amidships on either side.

**snag**—An underwater obstacle, often a sunken tree trunk.

**stern-wheeler**—A steamship whose paddle wheel is located at the stern.

**stowaway**—Someone who hides aboard a ship to avoid paying for passage.

**tallow**—Hard fat obtained from the carcasses of cattle, sheep, or horses. Tallow is used in foodstuffs or in the making of candles, soap, and lubricants.

**Texas Rangers**—Members of a mounted police force first organized in 1835 to keep order on the frontier.

**trail drivers**—Cowboys who herd cattle long distances to the market where they will be sold.

**vaquero**—Spanish name for cowboy or ranch hand.

# Further Reading

## Books

Freedman, Russell. *In the Days of the Vaqueros: America's First True Cowboys*. New York: Clarion Books, 2001.

Isaacs, Sally Senzell. *Cattle Trails and Cowboys*. Chicago: Heinemann Library, 2004.

Newton, Michael. *The Texas Rangers*. New York: Chelsea House Publishers, 2010.

Stanley, Jerry. *Cowboys & Longhorns*. New York: Crown Publishers, 2003.

Wade, Mary Dodson. *Henrietta King: La Patrona*. Houston, Tex.: Bright Sky Press, 2012.

## Internet Addresses

**Famous Texans: Richard King**

<http://www.famoustexans.com/RichardKing.htm>

**King Ranch**

<http://king-ranch.com/legacy_overview.html>

**Texas Ranch House: The Vaquero Origins of the Texas Cowboy**

<http://www.pbs.org/wnet/ranchhouse/1867_essay1.html>

# Index